This book
belongs to

....

....

ORCHARD BOOKS

First published in Great Britain in 2018 by The Watts Publishing Group

1 3 5 7 9 10 8 6 4 2

HASBRO and its logo, MY LITTLE PONY and all related characters are
trademarks of Hasbro and are used with permission.

MY LITTLE PONY: THE MOVIE © 2018 My Little Pony Productions, LLC.

Written by Sarah Levison

A CIP catalogue record for this book is available from the British Library

ISBN 978 1 40835 390 5

Printed and bound in China

MIX
Paper from
responsible sources
FSC
www.fsc.org   FSC® C104740

Orchard Books
An imprint of Hachette Children's Group
Part of The Watts Publishing Group Limited
Carmelite House
50 Victoria Embankment
London EC4Y 0DZ

An Hachette UK Company
www.hachette.co.uk

www.hachettechildrens.co.uk

Adult supervision is recommended for all
baking and cooking activities, and when
glue, paint, scissors and other
sharp points are in use.

Contents

Welcome!

Hello, friend! Thanks for joining us in our all-new awesome annual!

We're so pleased you're here to enjoy stories, activities, quizzes, colouring, jokes, crafts ... and so much more. You'll catch up with some familiar fillies (and some sneaky foes). Plus you'll have an exclusive sneak peek at some new areas of Equestria!

Love, hugs and high
hoof-bumps forever,

Twilight Sparkle,
Rainbow Dash, Rarity,
Applejack, Fluttershy,
Pinkie Pie and Spike!
x x x x x x

Who's Who?

We're sure you know lots about the ponies but we wanted to introduce the Mane Six. Here's all you need to know about the ponies bringing pal power to Equestria.

Princess Twilight Sparkle

Lives: In the Castle of Friendship
Pony Personality: Clever, kind, loyal, organised
Cutie Mark: Pink sparkle
Need to know ...
* Princess Celestia sent Twilight to Ponyville to learn about the magic of friendship. Here she met her five best friends!
* Twilight became a princess after using her great understanding of friendship to complete an ancient spell.
* Twilight is determined to share her knowledge so she set up the School of Friendship to unify all creatures and kingdoms!

Rainbow Dash

Lives: In the Clouds above Ponyville
Pony Personality: Fun, loyal, competitive, mischievous
Cutie Mark: Cloud and rainbow lightning bolt
Need to know ...
* It's Rainbow Dash's job to look after the weather in Ponyville.
* Rainbow Dash idolises the fast-flying Wonderbolts and was so excited when she finally earned a place on the team.
* Dash loves to play pranks – she's the joker of the pack!

Pinkie Pie

Lives: Above Sugarcube Corner, Ponyville's best bakery

Pony Personality: Energetic, zany, fun, kind, welcoming

Cutie Mark: Three balloons

Need to know ...

* As well as living above Sugarcube Corner, Pinkie also helps out in the shop.
* Although Pinkie can sometimes be a little kooky, she is sometimes the surprise voice of reason.
* Pinkie Pie organises the BEST parties in Equestria!

Fluttershy

Lives: In a cottage on the edge of the Everfree Forest

Pony Personality: Sweet, shy, sensitive, kind

Cutie Mark: Three pretty butterflies

Need to know ...

* Fluttershy is a Pegasus pony but she prefers to keep her hooves on the ground!
* Fluttershy lives with lots of animal friends, including birds, mice and rabbits.
* Although Fluttershy is kind and gentle, if you mess with any of her friends you'll be in big trouble!

Rarity

Lives: Above the fashionable Carousel Boutique

Pony Personality: Elegant, generous, honest, sweet

Cutie Mark: Three diamonds

Need to know ...

* Rarity is super-stylish but she's not just interested in how a pony looks on the outside – she cares about what's inside, too.
* Rarity owns shops in Canterlot and Manehattan but she lives in Ponyville so she's close to her friends.
* Rarity has a little sister called Sweetie Belle.

Applejack

Lives: At Sweet Apple Acres with her tight-knit family

Pony Personality: Kind, down-to-earth, hardworking, honest

Cutie Mark: Three red apples

Need to know ...

* Applejack will do anything for her friends and you can always count on her to lend a hoof or four!
* Applejack just loves her Stetson-style hat and you'll rarely see her without it.
* The farm is hard work but Applejack will always find time to hang out with her family and friends.

Creative Colouring

Now it's time to create a perfect picture with your favourite pony pals! Use your pens or pencils to colour in the picture. You could use glitter pens to really make them sparkle!

The Most Magical Map

It might look like a normal map but the friendship map is something quite special!

When Twilight Sparkle and her friends sat on their new thrones in the Castle of Friendship, their cutie marks glowed and a magical map appeared before them. They realised that the map was showing them friendship problems in Equestria.

Sometimes all of the ponies are needed to solve a problem, sometimes only one or two. When a pony is needed, their cutie mark glows and hovers over the map.

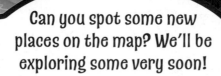

Can you spot some new places on the map? We'll be exploring some very soon!

CLUE: Look towards the bottom!

Rarity and Applejack were called to Manehattan to help their friend Coco Pommel. They helped her put on a play to bring the local community together!

The map is kept here, in Twilight's Castle of Friendship.

Twilight and Fluttershy were summoned to the Smoky Mountains to bring two warring tribes together.

Pinkie Pie and Rainbow Dash travelled to Griffonstone. They soon realised that the griffons were in desperate need of some friendship lessons!

School Daze

THE FRIENDSHIP MAP GREW TO INCLUDE MANY KINGDOMS BEYOND EQUESTRIA AND TWILIGHT SOON REALISED THAT ALL CREATURES NEEDED TO LEARN ABOUT THE MAGIC OF FRIENDSHIP. SHE DECIDED TO OPEN A SCHOOL OF FRIENDSHIP WHERE ALL CREATURES COULD LEARN TOGETHER! TWILIGHT WOULD BE THE HEADTEACHER AND HER BEST FRIENDS WOULD TEACH LESSONS, SHARING THEIR FRIENDSHIP EXPERIENCES WITH THE STUDENTS.

PRINCESS CELESTIA AGREED THAT THE SCHOOL OF FRIENDSHIP WAS A WONDERFUL IDEA, BUT THE PLANS WOULD NEED APPROVING BY THE EEA – THE EQUESTRIA EDUCATION ASSOCIATION.

"IF WE WANT TO KEEP OUR LAND SAFE, AND CREATE A FRIENDLIER TOMORROW, WE NEED TO TEACH THE MAGIC OF FRIENDSHIP FAR AND WIDE," TWILIGHT EXPLAINED TO CHANCELLOR NEIGHSAY. HE GAVE PERMISSION FOR THE SCHOOL TO OPEN!

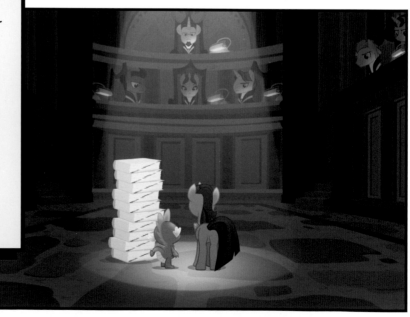

A FEW WEEKS LATER AND THE SCHOOL OF FRIENDSHIP WAS READY. THE DOORS OPENED AND THE FIRST STUDENTS ENTERED. AS WELL AS PONIES THERE WAS A GRIFFON, A CHANGELING, A HIPPOGRIFF, A YAK AND A DRAGON.

STUDENTS HAVE TRAVELLED FAR AND WIDE TO COME TO THE SCHOOL!

OVER THE NEXT FEW WEEKS THE STUDENTS ATTENDED MANY LESSONS. TWILIGHT'S FRIENDS TRIED THEIR BEST TO TEACH ACCORDING TO THE EEA'S RULES BUT IT WASN'T EASY.

"THERE'S NOT AN EQUATION ON HOW TO HAVE FUN!" SAID PINKIE PIE. THE OTHERS WERE ALSO STRUGGLING WITH HOW TO BEST SHARE THEIR FRIENDSHIP EXPERIENCES. MEANWHILE, THE STUDENTS WERE GETTING VERY BORED!

SINCE THE STUDENTS WEREN'T HAVING FUN, THEY STARTED TO SQUABBLE AND FIGHT.

"WE NEED TO TRY SOMETHING NEW," STARLIGHT GLIMMER TOLD TWILIGHT LATER THAT DAY.

"NO, THE SCHOOL HAS TO FOLLOW THE RULES OF THE EEA!" CRIED TWILIGHT SPARKLE.

BUT THE STUDENTS WERE SO BORED THAT A GROUP OF THEM DECIDED TO MISS THAT MORNING'S LESSONS AND HAVE FUN INSTEAD ...

CHANCELLOR NEIGHSAY CAME TO CHECK ON THE SCHOOL. BUT SIX STUDENTS WERE MISSING!

THEY WERE ENJOYING THEMSELVES FOR THE FIRST TIME SINCE SCHOOL STARTED. BUT WHEN OCELLUS THE CHANGELING TRANSFORMED INTO A MONSTER AND WAS SPOTTED BY CHANCELLOR NEIGHSAY – CHAOS BROKE OUT! "THE SCHOOL IS UNDER ATTACK!" SHOUTED THE PANICKED PONY.

YOUR SCHOOL IS A DISASTER! BY ORDER OF THE EEA, THIS SCHOOL IS CLOSED!

A HUGE FIGHT BROKE OUT WITH EVERYONE BLAMING EACH OTHER FOR THE STUDENTS' BEHAVIOUR. THE NEW STUDENTS DECIDED TO LEAVE THE SCHOOL. TWILIGHT SPARKLE WAS FURIOUS ... BUT NOPONY WAS AS ANGRY AS CHANCELLOR NEIGHSAY.

TWILIGHT WAS DEVASTATED! "I'M SUPPOSED TO BE THE PRINCESS OF FRIENDSHIP," SHE WAILED. "ALL I DID WAS MAKE ENEMIES AND UPSET MY FRIENDS!"

"YOU'VE GIVEN UP TOO EASILY!" STARLIGHT GLIMMER SAID. "WHY SHOULD YOU LET SOMEPONY ELSE STOP YOU FROM DOING YOUR JOB? YOU NEED TO WRITE YOUR OWN RULES BECAUSE YOU'RE DOING SOMETHING NEW AND IMPORTANT."

TWILIGHT REALISED HER FRIEND WAS RIGHT.

"I SHOULD HAVE LISTENED TO YOU ALL, I'M SORRY. THIS TIME WE'LL RUN THE SCHOOL TOGETHER!" BUT SPIKE POINTED OUT A LITTLE PROBLEM ... THE FIVE STUDENTS FROM THE OTHER KINGDOMS – YONA, SMOLDER, OCELLUS, SILVERSTREAM AND GALLUS – WOULD NEED TO BE PERSUADED TO COME BACK TO SCHOOL.

THE FRIENDS SET OFF TO BRING BACK THE NON-PONY STUDENTS BUT THEY HAD ALL GONE MISSING ... TOGETHER! TWILIGHT KNEW SHE HAD TO FIND THEM SOON OR ALL THE KINGDOMS WOULD BE AT WAR.

THE FRIENDS SUSPECTED SANDBAR KNEW WHERE THE OTHERS WERE. THEY DECIDED TO FOLLOW HIM AND SEE IF HE WOULD LEAD THEM TO THE OTHERS.

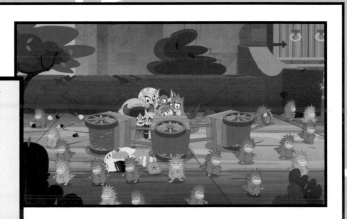

WHEN THE STUDENTS WERE ATTACKED BY A GROUP OF ANGRY PUCKWUDGIES, THEY WERE IN BIG TROUBLE! LUCKILY, THE TEACHERS FOUGHT OFF THE CREATURES.

"YOU HAVE STARTED TO LEARN ABOUT FRIENDSHIP," SAID TWILIGHT. "BUT WE'D LIKE YOU TO COME BACK TO SCHOOL. THINGS WILL BE DIFFERENT THIS TIME!"

THE STUDENTS AGREED TO COME BACK TO SCHOOL. BUT CHANCELLOR NEIGHSAY TRIED TO FORBID THE SCHOOL FROM REOPENING! HEADTEACHER TWILIGHT WAS READY FOR HIM. "THIS IS A FRIENDSHIP SCHOOL WITH ITS OWN RULES. MY SCHOOL IS GOING TO DO THINGS DIFFERENTLY!"

CHANCELLOR NEIGHSAY BACKED DOWN AND THE SCHOOL OF FRIENDSHIP REOPENED WITH ALL STUDENTS AND TEACHERS ENJOYING THE WONDERFUL MAGIC OF FRIENDSHIP TOGETHER!

THE END

The School of Friendship

Twilight Sparkle's new school is the first of its kind in Equestria. Let's take a closer look!

The school is painted in Twilight's colours – shades of purple and pink. The school flag also features her cutie mark.

The school is next to the Castle of Friendship, so it's only a short trot for Headteacher Twilight Sparkle to get to work each day!

If you look closely you'll spot a crest featuring six gems, each representing an Element of Harmony. These six elements (honesty, loyalty, generosity, laughter, kindness and magic) are at the heart of the School of Friendship.

When students enter the school they come into the magnificent entrance hall. Here there are statues of wise and brave ponies from Equestria's ancient past.

Each teacher has a unique classroom … can you guess who teaches in this party popping room? It's Pinkie Pie, of course. She is the teacher of laughter and fun!

Twilight's office is fit for a royal Headteacher! In this peaceful space Twilight can focus on running the school. A huge clock above her desk makes sure she is never late for those all-important meetings.

At the centre of the School of Friendship is this peaceful courtyard. Here, students can gather to catch up with friends. After all, every creature needs friends!

The New School Crew

The School of Friendship is very special because it's open to all creatures from the lands surrounding Equestria. Here's a guide to some of the new kids in school!

Silverstream

* Silverstream is a Hippogriff and Queen Novo's niece.

* This chatty Seapony spent most of her life underwater in her aunt's kingdom! After the Mane Six freed her and her family, she was able to return to the skies once again.

* Silverstream is so excited to be at the School of Friendship. She can't wait to get to know everyone and start learning all about friendship!

Yona

* Yona the Yak is from Yakyakistan (a kingdom to the far north of Equestria).

* Yaks are very proud of their history and heritage. Yona thinks Yakyakistan is the best place in the world.

* Yaks are huge! Even though Yona is only young, she is already pretty big … and she's only going to get bigger!

Gallus

∗ Gallus is a young Griffon and the grandson of Grandpa Gruff.
∗ Gallus comes from Griffonstone, to the east of Equestria.
∗ At first, Gallus isn't sure he has a lot to learn at school as he is already so confident.

Ocellus

∗ Ocellus is a Changeling – she can use her magic to change form.
∗ When she first comes to school Ocellus changes into a Dragon and confuses Spike!
∗ Ocellus is very shy and changes form to hide from others. But when she gets to know the other students she is happy to stay as herself.

Smolder

∗ Smolder the Dragon is from the Dragonlands.
∗ Smolder has travelled all the way across the Celestial Sea. Luckily, Dragons are strong fliers!
∗ At first Smolder doesn't want to be at the school but she is ordered to attend.

Sandbar

∗ The only Pony in the group, Sandbar is very laid back.
∗ Sandbar soon becomes good friends with the non-pony pupils despite their differences.

Rainbow Dash's Happy Days Decoration

Rainbow Dash is surrounded by clouds of all shapes and sizes in Cloudsdale and now it's time for you to have one, too!

You will need:
- A sheet of white felt or card
- A pencil
- A pair of scissors
- 5 lengths of ribbon, approximately 20cm long
- PVA glue
- Small pom-poms in various colours
- A grown-up to help

1
Draw a cloud shape on to your felt or card using a pencil.

2
Ask a grown-up to help you cut out the shape.

3

Stick four pieces of ribbon to the back of the cloud shape using PVA glue. Leave to dry.

4

Carefully stick the pom-poms onto the lengths of ribbon using PVA glue. Leave to dry.

5

Stick the final ribbon to the top of the cloud in a loop – this will be used to hang your cloud. Leave to dry.

You don't have to use white felt or card – you can make clouds of all colours of the rainbow!

6

If you like, draw a smiley face on your cloud. Now it's ready to hang up!

All About You!

It's time for the ponies to get the low down on a VVIP (Very Very Important Person) – that's you! So choose your favourite pen or pencil and fill in your details below.

Fast Facts

Name **Evie**

Age **9**

Eye colour **Hazle**

Hair colour **blound**

Where I live **near piperhill**

Best friend **Lexi**

Pet **two cats and some chicks chickens**

It's all about the dragons!

Would you rather?

Circle which answer you would choose

Eat an ice cream **OR** a pizza?

Go flying with Rainbow Dash **OR** plan a party with Pinkie Pie?

Wear a pink top **OR** a yellow top?

Design a dress with Rarity **OR** practise magic with Twilight Sparkle?

Play with a puppy **OR** a kitten?

Lie on a beach **OR** go for a walk?

Make an apple pie with Applejack **OR** have a picnic with Fluttershy?

Hang out with the Cutie Mark Crusaders **OR** visit dragons with Spike?

Pick Six!

Choose six words that best describe you

- ☑ HAPPY
- ☐ CONFIDENT
- ☑ FRIENDLY
- ☑ FUN
- ☐ LOYAL
- ☑ SWEET
- ☑ SHY

- ☑ SMILEY
- ☐ QUIET
- ☐ LOUD
- ☐ POPULAR
- ☐ CLEVER
- ☐ SPORTY
- ☐ STRONG

Fantastic Family
Draw or stick in a picture of your family

My Favourite Things

Food _sweets/chocolate_

Drink _fanta orange_

Animal _kittens, puppies bunny_

Book _my little pony_

Colour _pink_

My Little Pony _mane six_

Fruit _straberys_

Favourite fruit? It's gotta be an apple!

Pick me! Pick me!

25

Super Starlight

Starlight Glimmer has had an amazing journey from sneaky stranger to Twilight's star pupil. Here's all you need to know!

1 Starlight ruled a strange village where everypony had the same Cutie Mark. When the Mane Six refused to give theirs up, Starlight made them her prisoners!

2 Starlight used a time spell to travel back in time and stop Rainbow Dash performing her first sonic rainboom. This changed Equestria's history for the worse!

3 Starlight finally admitted that when she was a filly, her friend Sunburst had moved away and she was afraid to make new friends.

4 Instead of punishing Starlight, Twilight decided to teach her about the magic of friendship!

EVILOMETER

5 Starlight met her old friend Sunburst. The two apologised for losing touch and worked together to save the Crystal Empire!

6 Starlight made friends with Trixie. But when Trixie admitted she only wanted to be close to Twilight, Starlight was hurt. After apologising, the two became firm friends.

7 When changelings captured the royal princesses, Starlight used her friendship lessons to save Equestria!

8 Starlight was awarded the Pink Heart of Courage and is now a true friend to all in Equestria. Hurrah!

Spot the Difference

Starlight and Sunburst were best friends when they were little and now they are friends again! Can you spot five differences between the two pictures?

A

Answer on page 62

Circle the changes when you find them!

B

Fashion Fun

Hello darlings! I think about fashion almost all of the time. Can you spot eight fabulously fashionable words in the grid below?

☑ DESIGN ☑ GARMENT ☑ FABRIC ☑ BOUTIQUE ☑ TASSEL ☑ BUTTON ☑ ZIP ☑ LACE

Z	D	E	S	I	G	N	P
P	I	U	G	E	U	B	T
C	P	P	A	N	S	U	A
F	A	B	R	I	C	T	S
X	C	A	M	E	C	T	S
L	A	C	E	R	N	O	E
L	K	E	N	T	A	N	L
B	O	U	T	I	Q	U	E

Look carefully, they could be anywhere!

Answer on page 62

Tidy up Time!

Uh oh! Rarity has had a busy day in the boutique and she needs your help to get everything in order. Count up the items and write the number in the box.

6 Hats
1 Handbags
2 Sunglasses
4 Bows
2 Spools of Thread

Answer on page 62

Princess Celestia's Helper

Princess Celestia needs help solving a friendship problem.
Read the list below and tick the pony she has chosen to help.

1. The pony must love books

2. The pony will be a unicorn

3. The pony must have natural magical abilities

4. The pony will love dragons

5. The pony must be willing to learn important friendship lessons

6. The pony will, in time, become a teacher herself ...

Answer on page 62

Discord's Dastardly Jokes

Discord loves to play tricks and pranks on his friends. Here are some of his favourite jokes!

Q: What do you get if you cross a frog with a rabbit?

A: A bunny ribbit!

Q: What is black and white and eats like a horse?

A: A zebra

Person 1: Knock-knock.

Person 2: Who's there?

Person 1: Cow says.

Person 2: Cow says who?

Person 1: No, silly! A cow says 'Mooooo!'

Q: Why did the banana go to the hospital?

A: He was peeling really bad.

Q: How many tickles does it take to get an octopus to laugh?

A: Ten-tickles

Q: Why was 6 afraid of 7?

A: Because 7, 8, 9!

Q: What is the difference between a unicorn and a carrot?

A: One is a funny beast and the other is a bunny feast.

Q: What street do ponies live on?

A: Mane Street

HA! HA! HA! HAHA! HA! HA! HA! HAHA!

32

Discord's Date Delights

Discord didn't have any friends until Fluttershy showed him true kindness, so he has decided to make some delicious treats for her. Why not make these healthy treats for your friends and family?

Makes 12 treats
You will need:
- Food processor or knife
- 100g soft dates (pitted)
- 50g soft dried apricots
- 50g dried cranberries
- Glass bowl
- One tablespoon of desiccated coconut
- Small plate
- A grown-up to help

1 Tip all of the dried fruit into a food processor.

2 Ask a grown-up to whizz the fruit until it is finely chopped. If you don't have a food processor, the fruit can be chopped finely with a knife.

3 Tip the mixture into a glass bowl and squeeze together.

4 Roll the mixture into twelve small balls, then roll on a plate in the desiccated coconut.

5 Store in an airtight container. The treats will last for 3-4 days.

Under the Sea

Twilight and her friends stumbled across Seaquestria by accident and they are so glad they did. Not only is it exciting to have a new land to explore but they've also made some amazing new friends.

From Land to Sea

The Hippogriffs originally lived on Mount Aris, an island south of mainland Equestria. The Storm King tried to capture the Hippogriffs and make them his slaves. Queen Novo used a magical pearl to change her subjects into Seaponies so they could live safely beneath the waves. But although the Hippogriffs lived peacefully in the deep ocean, they longed to return to their home and fly high in the skies once again …

Royal Princess

Queen Novo has a daughter called Princess Skystar. When Twilight and her friends came to Seaquestria, Princess Skystar was so excited to have fun with them!

Powerful Pearl

A gleaming pearl is the source of the Hippogriffs' power. Queen Novo keeps this in her throne room. The queen turned the Hippogriffs into Seaponies by harnessing the magic of the pearl.

Underwater fun!

Queen Novo turned Twilight and her friends into underwater creatures! The friends loved being able to explore beneath the waves. Rainbow Dash was as fast under the water as above it, and Pinkie Pie threw an ocean party to cheer up Princess Skystar.

A Sinister Storm ...

The Storm King was desperate to rule Equestria. He had incredible power at his fingertips – he could create tornadoes and control thunder and lightning! He also had armies of creatures to help him, including mysterious mare Tempest and her sidekick, Grubber. Luckily, Twilight and her friends were able to defeat the Storm King and the Hippogriffs were free to return to their home above water.

Pretty as a Picture

Elegant Queen Novo is the regal ruler of the Seaponies! Can you complete this picture using your pens or pencils?

Story Time

Isn't it exciting to meet new friends! Write a short story about the Seaponies and the underwater fun of your pony friends.

You can use these phrases to help you!

- The mean Storm King
- Thunder and lightning
- A magical underwater world
- Zooming through the water
- The power of friendship
- Spike the puffer fish
- Twilight Sparkle and her friends
- Happily ever after

Once upon a time, in the amazing world of Seaquestria ...

_____
_____
_____
_____
_____
_____
_____
_____
_____
_____
_____
_____
_____
_____
_____
_____

The Name Game

What would your Pony name be? Hold your finger above the first box, close your eyes and let your finger rest on a name. Repeat for each box then put them together to make a magical new name!

Princess	Sparkle	Hooves
Night	Shimmer	Heart
Dream	Star Shine	Mane
Bubble	Dance	Tail
Precious	Spin	Smile
Magic	Rainbow	Flower

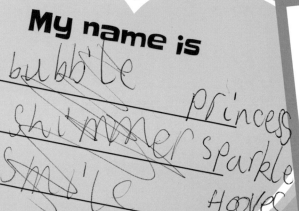

My name is

bubble princess

shimmer sparkle

smile hooves

My Cutie Mark will look like this

Home Sweet Home

Applejack has been harvesting apples all day and wants to go home for a well-deserved rest. Can you help her find the quickest route through the orchard?

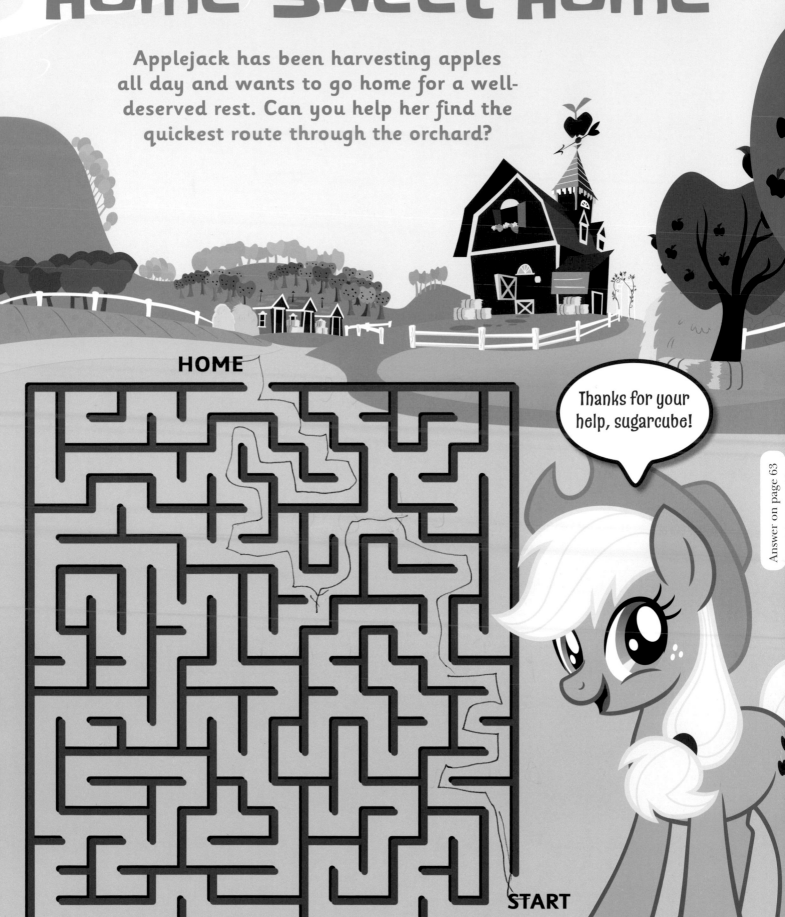

HOME

Thanks for your help, sugarcube!

START

Answer on page 63

Party Time with Pinkie Pie!

Pinkie Pie is planning an awesome party for Starlight Glimmer but she's got into a bit of a muddle. Can you help her by unscrambling the four party words below?

A E C K
cake

L A B O O L N
balloon

S E P N R E T
present

D I N C A N G
dancing

Answers on page 63

Pinkie's Party Picture

Pinkie Pie looks a little lonely in this picture. Can you use your best drawing skills to add some party accessories? Then colour in the picture and let the fun begin!

Rarity's Daring 'Dos

Rarity loves to change her look depending on where she is and what she's up to. Here's a closer look at some of her sensational styles. Why don't you try creating your own gorgeous hair-dos?

1 Wondrous Waves

This is a classic daytime look for Rarity – simple, chic and oh-so-elegant!
Rarity's hair has a natural curl, so to achieve this look she simply spritzes her mane and tail with a little hairspray and then tidies with a wide-toothed comb. Perfection!

3 One to Wow!

Although Rarity usually keeps it classic, on occasion she knows how to surprise with a daring dramatic style! To create this particular look, Rarity curls her mane using rollers. Then she accessorises the curls with bright feathers and a jeweled hairband. Breathtaking!

2 Up and Elegant

Rarity showcases this look on formal occasions, such as weddings or balls. To create this style Rarity scoops up a large section of her mane and secures it at the back of her head using hair grips. She then backcombs the rest in sections and tucks it in at the front.

Twilight's Test

Twilight prides herself on having an excellent memory, but now it's your turn! Study the scene for twenty seconds, then cover it with a piece of paper and answer the questions below.

Remember, no peeping!

1 Who is Twilight hugging on the stage?

_____

2 Which Pegasus pony is hovering in the air on the left of the picture?

_____

3 What is on the purple banner above the stage?

_____

4 Does Trixie's hat have stars or moons?

_____

Answers on page 63

Fluttershy's Gorgeous Garden

Fluttershy is never happier than when she's in her beautiful cottage garden, surrounded by nature. Create a magical mini garden for your home!

You will need:
- A sturdy and waterproof container, such as a washing-up bowl or plant pot
- Sand or gravel
- Soil
- A selection of small plants
- Pebbles or shells to decorate
- A small plastic dish for a pond (optional)
- Accessories such as doll's house furniture or tiny toys (optional)
- A grown-up to help

Fluttershy's Top Tips:
- Choose small plants that won't grow too large for your mini garden!

- Decide if your garden will be kept indoors or outdoors and choose plants to fit.

- Remember to water your garden regularly to keep it looking beautiful!

1

Cover the base of your container with a layer of sand or gravel to help drainage.

2

Fill your container with soil.

3

Plan the design of your garden before you start planting. A grown-up can help with this!

4

Carefully place the plants in your garden and top up with soil.

5

Decorate with pebbles or shells. You could even make a little path!

6

Add any finishing touches to your garden. Why not add a little pond to fill with water? Or a doll's house bench or table could be the perfect spot for a passing Breezie to rest on!

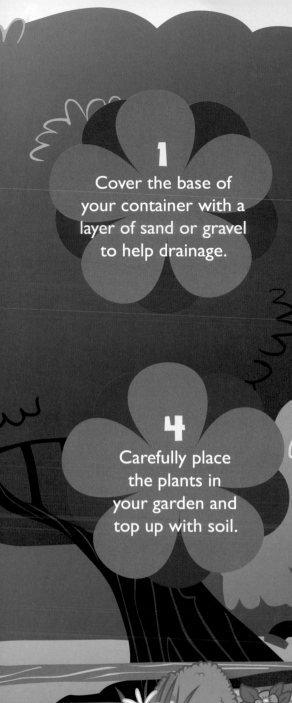

Take the Test!

How well do you know the world of Equestria?
Answer the questions to see how in-the-know you are!

1
Who lives here?
a Rainbow Dash
b Zecora
c Apple Bloom

2
Where did Pinkie Pie live and work before she moved to Ponyville?
a A rock farm
b A confetti factory
c A carrot farm

3
Who is the new leader of the changelings?
a Lorax
b Thorax
c Sparkle Wing

4
Which pony helped Discord change his tricksy ways?
a Fluttershy
b Pinkie Pie
c Starlight Glimmer

5
Who sent Twilight Sparkle to Ponyville?
a Princess Cadance
b Princess Luna
c Princess Celestia

46

6
What is the name of this castle?

a Castle of Forgetfulness
b Castle of Friendship
c Castle of Fun

7
What is Rarity's little sister called?

a Sweetie Treatie
b Sweetie Cheeks
c Sweetie Belle

8
What type of animal is Fluttershy's companion?

a Mouse
b Bunny
c Bear

9
Who did Princess Luna transform into?

a Fluttershy
b Discord
c Nightmare Moon

10
Who is the Captain of the Wonderbolts

a Spitfire
b Slow Coach
c So Fast

How did you score?

0-3
Uh oh! You need to brush up on your pony facts. You're sure to have lots of fun learning about your new friends.

4-7
Well done – you really know your Equestria trivia. Keep up the good work pony pals!

8-10
Wow you're a pony expert! Give yourself a pat on the back and a high hoof bump. You're a true fan!

Answers: 1) b 2) a 3) b 4) a 5) c 6) b 7) c 8) b 9) c 10) a

The Baddest of Them All ...

The pony friends have had to deal with some fearsome foes on their adventures. Each enemy has their own scary strengths and terrible tactics ... but which one do you think is the meanest?

The Queen of Mean

Queen Chrysalis trapped Princess Cadance in a dungeon and transformed to look like Cadance. Her plan was to marry Shining Armor and take over Equestria. Luckily, Twilight and her friends managed to free the real Princess Cadance and banish Queen Chrysalis. But that wasn't the end of her! Next she captured all of the powerful ponies in Equestria, and Discord, Trixie and Starlight Glimmer had to rescue them!

MEANIE MARK OUT OF 10

$\dfrac{10}{10}$

Stormy Seas

The Storm King was one fierce foe. He had the power to harness thunder and create terrifying tornadoes! He was desperate to rule all of Equestria and wouldn't let anypony stand in his way … even forcing the Hippogriffs to hide in the ocean. Twilight and her friends freed the Hippogriffs and taught him a lesson using the powerful magic of friendship.

MEANIE MARK OUT OF 10

$\frac{8}{10}$

Terrible Tirek

This giant Centaur is one seriously scary creature. Lord Tirek was supposed to be imprisoned in Tartarus, but he escaped and made himself more powerful by stealing others' magic! Twilight Sparkle fought Tirek but won the battle when she chose to free her friends rather than keep her magic. This sacrifice led to Tirek losing his magic and being imprisoned once again. Phew!

MEANIE MARK OUT OF 10

$\frac{}{10}$

Dastardly Discord

Discord is one tricksy Draconequus! He's always getting into mischief and causing trouble. But after Fluttershy showed him what true friendship was all about, this fickle fiend changed his ways. He even joined forces with Starlight Glimmer and Trixie to rescue the Mane Six from Queen Chrysalis!

MEANIE MARK OUT OF 10

$\frac{5}{10}$

Fake it 'Til you Make it

FLUTTERSHY AND HER ANIMAL FRIENDS WERE ENJOYING A PEACEFUL PICNIC ON A SUNNY AFTERNOON. SUDDENLY THE PEACE WAS DISTURBED BY RARITY – AND SHE WAS IN A REAL PANIC! IT WAS ALMOST TIME FOR THE CANTERLOT FASHION SHOW AND RARITY REALLY NEEDED SOMEPONY TO LOOK AFTER HER BOUTIQUE, RARITY FOR YOU.

FLUTTERSHY WAS HAPPY TO HELP, EVEN THOUGH THE THOUGHT OF HELPING IN A BUSY SHOP MADE HER FEEL ANXIOUS.

RARITY'S MANEHATTAN BOUTIQUE WAS VERY FANCY. FLUTTERSHY TRIED TO HELP A CUSTOMER BUT IT WASN'T EASY. "YOU SIMPLY MUST ACCESS YOUR INNER STRENGTH!" ADVISED RARITY. WHEN RARITY LEFT FLUTTERSHY IN CHARGE, THE SHY PONY PUT ON A SMART SUIT AND ADOPTED A POSH VOICE. THE SNOOTY CUSTOMERS SEEMED TO LIKE IT!

SOON FLUTTERSHY AND RARITY'S RACCOON HELPERS WERE VERY BUSY IN THE BOUTIQUE. IN FACT, FLUTTERSHY WAS HAVING FUN! BEFORE LONG SHE CHANGED HER OUTFIT AND ATTITUDE TO SUIT EVERY CUSTOMER THAT CAME IN ... ONE MINUTE SHE WAS POSH AND THE NEXT MINUTE GOTH! AS A RESULT, FLUTTERSHY SOLD LOTS OF CLOTHES AND ACCESSORIES TO THE DIFFERENT CUSTOMERS.

THIS OUTFIT IS, LIKE, TOTALLY YOU.

A JACKET IS ONLY A JACKET IF IT'S BLACK.

BUT FLUTTERSHY WAS TRYING SO HARD TO PLEASE EVERYPONY THAT SHE FORGOT TO LOOK AFTER THE RACCOON HELPERS, EVEN THOUGH THEY WERE WORKING VERY HARD. WHEN FLUTTERSHY WAS RUDE TO HER FURRY FRIENDS, THEY VISITED TWILIGHT SPARKLE TO TELL HER WHAT WAS GOING ON.

"I CAN'T IMAGINE FLUTTERSHY WOULD EVER BE MEAN," WORRIED TWILIGHT. "THIS SOUNDS SERIOUS ..."

TWILIGHT SPARKLE, APPLEJACK, RAINBOW DASH AND PINKIE PIE WENT TO VISIT THE BOUTIQUE. THEY TRIED TO TALK TO FLUTTERSHY BUT SHE WOULDN'T LISTEN ... AND SHE WOULDN'T STOP PRETENDING TO BE DIFFERENT SORTS OF PONIES!

"LOOK, FLUTTERSHY," SAID TWILIGHT, "THERE'S GOT TO BE A BETTER WAY!" BUT FLUTTERSHY LOCKED TWILIGHT AND HER FRIENDS OUT OF THE SHOP. WHAT WERE THEY GOING TO DO NOW?

IN CANTERLOT, RARITY WAS IN THE MIDDLE OF HER CATWALK SHOW. BUT WHEN SHE HEARD WHAT WAS GOING ON AT THE BOUTIQUE SHE RACED BACK STRAIGHT AWAY. THINGS HAD GONE FROM BAD TO WORSE. FLUTTERSHY HAD TAKEN HER ROLE-PLAY SO FAR THAT NOW SHE WAS OFFENDING THE CUSTOMERS!

"THIS IS WORSE THAN I COULD POSSIBLY HAVE IMAGINED!" RARITY GASPED.

RARITY DECIDED THERE WAS ONLY ONE THING FOR IT ... SHE HAD TO FIRE FLUTTERSHY! THANKFULLY THIS BROUGHT FLUTTERSHY TO HER SENSES AND SHE APOLOGISED TO THE PONIES AND THE RACOONS FOR HER RUDE BEHAVIOUR.

"I WAS JUST TRYING TO PLEASE EVERYPONY," SHE EXPLAINED. "ACTING LIKE THE SNOOTY CUSTOMERS GAVE ME THE CONFIDENCE TO HELP THEM."

I'M SORRY, RARITY!

RARITY GAVE FLUTTERSHY A HUG. "YOU HAVE ALL THE INNER STRENGTH YOU NEED. BUT I THINK IT'S BETTER WHEN IT COMES FROM OUR REGULAR, SWEET FLUTTERSHY!" THEN RARITY HAD A FLASH OF INSPIRATION. HER COLLECTION WAS MISSING ITS STAR DRESS, AND NOW RARITY KNEW EXACTLY WHAT IT SHOULD LOOK LIKE ...

YOU'VE GIVEN ME THE MOST FABULOUS IDEA!

A FEW DAYS LATER IT WAS TIME TO SHOWCASE RARITY'S NEW DRESS 'THE WARRIOR OF INNER STRENGTH' AND THERE WAS ONLY ONE PONY RARITY WANTED TO MODEL IT ... FLUTTERSHY!

"OH IT'S LOVELY RARITY," SMILED FLUTTERSHY. "I'M JUST SO SORRY YOU MISSED THE END OF YOUR FASHION SHOW."

"DON'T WORRY, MAKING THE PERFECT DRESS IS VERY SATISFYING," REASSURED RARITY.

WHEN A SNOOTY FASHION REPORTER ASKED WHY RARITY DIDN'T SHOW THE DRESS AT FASHION WEEK FLUTTERSHY DEFENDED HER FRIEND AND PUT THE REPORTER FIRMLY IN HER PLACE. RARITY SMILED WHEN SHE REALISED THAT FLUTTERSHY REALLY HAD FOUND HER INNER STRENGTH – AND NOW SHE WASN'T AFRAID TO USE IT!

THE END

Cutie Mark Crusaders' Clubhouse Treats

The Cutie Mark Crusaders are best friends. You can't go adventuring around Equestria on an empty stomach, so here are three of their favourite recipes for making together.

Sweetie Belle's Beautiful Biscuits

1 Pre-heat the oven to 180°c/160°c fan.

2 Mix the butter and sugar together with a wooden spoon until light and fluffy.

3 Slowly add the egg and vanilla essence.

4 Add the sieved flour and salt. Mix together until it forms a thick dough.

5 Wrap the dough in clingfilm and chill in the fridge for at least 30 minutes.

6 Roll out the dough on a floured surface until it is approximately ½ cm thick.

7 Cut out your shapes with biscuit cutters.

8 Line a baking tray with greaseproof paper and place the biscuits on the tray.

9 Bake for 8-10 minutes or until golden brown.

10 Leave to cool.

Makes 15 biscuits
You will need:
- 85g unsalted butter, softened
- 100g caster sugar
- 1 large egg, beaten
- 1 teaspoon vanilla essence
- 200g self-raising flour (plus extra for rolling)
- ½ teaspoon salt
- Biscuit cutters
- A grown-up to help

Apple Bloom's Super Smoothie

**Makes 4 smoothies
You will need:**
- 250g frozen berries, such as raspberries, blueberries and strawberries
- Strawberry yoghurt
- 100ml milk
- 25g porridge oats
- Blender
- A grown-up to help

1 Ask a grown-up to put the berries, yoghurt and milk into a blender and mix together.

2 Stir through the porridge oats.

3 Pour into four glasses and serve.

4 If you like your smoothies super sweet, you could add a teaspoon of honey!

Scootaloo's Fruity Rockets

1 Wash and dry the fruit.

2 Carefully thread the blueberries and grapes onto the skewers, alternating the two fruits.

3 Top each skewer with a strawberry to make a point at the top of the rocket.

**Makes 6 rockets
You will need:**
- 12 seedless grapes
- 18 blueberries
- 6 strawberries
- 6 wooden skewers
- A grown-up to help

Your Gem Destiny

Spike loves gems as a super shiny snack but these sparkly jewels can also reveal something about you! Find the month you were born in to reveal your birthstone.

Gem power
* Luck * Health * Wealth

You are
* Positive
* Creative
* Popular

FEBRUARY
Amethyst

Gem power
* Patience * Peace * Courage

You are
* Generous
* Thoughtful
* Brave

MARCH
Aquamarine

Gem power
* Protection * Happiness
* Friendship

You are
* Confident
* Peaceful
* Fearless

A snack? What a terrible waste of such gorgeous jewels!

APRIL
Diamond

Gem power
* Healing * Love * Friendship

You are
* Strong
* Reliable
* Loyal

MAY
Emerald

Gem power
* Success * Peace
* Good sense

You are
* Helpful
* Sensitive
* Happy

JUNE
Pearl

Gem power
* Wisdom * Power * Peace

You are
* Honest
* Patient
* Calm

Gem power
* Luck * Friendship * Loyalty

You are
* Determined
* Headstrong
* Brave

AUGUST
Peridot

Gem power
* Luck * Health * Beauty

You are
* Happy
* Healthy
* Strong

SEPTEMBER
Sapphire

Gem power
* Wisdom * Loyalty * Discipline

You are
* Wise
* Focused
* Fun

OCTOBER
Opal

Gem power
* Imagination * Emotion
* Sensitivity

You are
* Energetic
* Spirited
* Loyal

NOVEMBER
Topaz

Gem power
* Soothing * Helps sleep
* Creativity

You are
* Imaginative
* Kind
* Calm

DECEMBER
Turquoise

Gem power
* Happiness * Victory
* Sensitivity

You are
* Popular
* Friendly
* Strong

Team Wonderbolt

The Wonderbolts are the fastest, most daring Pegasi ponies in Equestria. Rainbow Dash was so excited to finally make the team. Join the dots to finish their Cutie Mark and then colour in the team.

Wonderbolts' Wonderlist

Spitfire is the leader of the Wonderbolts – the fastest, most daring and bravest flying squad. Here's a bit more about what makes the Wonderbolts so special.

W is for **wow**. This sums us up!

O is for **out of this world**. Sometimes we fly so high we look down at all of Equestria.

N is for **noble**. The Wonderbolts have a noble past and we are an important part of Equestria's culture.

D is for **daredevil**. We're fearless fliers!

E is for **extraordinary**. Because we are!

R is for **Rainbow Dash**. The latest addition to our dream team.

B is for **Blaze**. A core member of the Wonderbolts.

O is for **organisation**. Spitfire always keeps the team organised and on track.

L is for **learning**. We learn new skills and train hard at the Wonderbolts Academy.

T is for **teamwork**. We work together as one unstoppable unit.

S is for **Sonic Rainboom**. The most amazing aerial move!

Try writing your own poem with your name!

Life Lessons

The School of Friendship has transformed the way students in Equestria learn about friendship. Here, the new students share a lesson they have learned since starting school.

I thought there was nothing the School of Friendship could teach me ... but I was wrong! I've learned that every pony and creature has something special to share with the world – you just have to listen and give them a chance.

Everyone is special!

Gallus

Silverstream

Yona

I love my home in Yakyakistan and felt very homesick when I first arrived at the school. Now I know that there's so much to see and explore in the world – and it makes going home even more special!

After spending a long time under the sea I was so excited to be at school and tried to do everything all at once! I've learned it's OK to relax sometimes. The most important lessons are learned when you aren't looking for them.

Ocellus

When I first started school I was very nervous. I changed the way I looked all the time to hide my true self and fit in with the crowd. I've learned to have confidence in who I am – now I'm not afraid to show the real me.

Be true to yourself!

I was a bit nervous about meeting lots of different creatures from all over Equestria – I didn't know if we'd get along! Now I know that it doesn't matter where you come from or what you look like – that's the magic of friendship.

Sandbar

Smolder

All dragons are competitive and when I first arrived at school I thought everything was a competition! I've learned that everyone is different and enjoys different things. You can't be the best at everything and that's OK!

The most important lesson is to keep learning!

61

Answers

Spot the Difference

Fashion Fun

Z	D	E	S	I	G	N	P
P	I	U	G	E	U	B	T
C	P	P	A	N	S	U	A
F	A	B	R	I	C	T	S
X	C	A	M	E	C	T	S
L	A	C	E	R	N	O	E
L	K	E	N	T	A	N	L
B	O	U	T	I	Q	U	E

Tidy Up Time!

- 6 Hats
- 1 Handbag
- 2 Sunglasses
- 4 Bows
- 2 Spools of Thread

Princess Celestia's Helper

Well done, darlings!

Home Sweet Home

HOME

Thanks for your help, sugarcube!

START

Party Time with Pinkie Pie!

CAKE

BALLOON

PRESENT

DANCING

Twilight's Test

1 Starlight Glimmer

2 Rainbow Dash

3 Love Heart

4 Stars

Explore the magical world of My Little Pony!

978 1 40834 293 0 — Creative Colouring Book

978 1 40834 945 8 — Magical Creative Colouring

978 1 40834 986 1 — Ultimate Creative Colouring

978 1 40835 027 0 — Super Sticker Scenes

978 1 40834 473 6 — Pinkie Pie's Party Sticker and Activity Book

978 1 40835 494 0 — Big Book of Activity Fun

978 1 40834 474 3 — Dress-Up Fun Sticker Activity Book

978 1 40834 752 2 — Bumper Wipe-Clean Activity Fun

978 1 40834 751 5 — Magical Sound Book

978 1 40835 064 5 — Ultimate Guide

Orchard books are available from all good bookshops.

ORCHARD